Lessons on Demand Presents

Teacher Guide and Novel Unit for Fish in a Tree

By: John Pennington

The lessons on demand series is designed to provide ready to use resources for novel study. In this book you will find key vocabulary, student organizer pages, and assessments.

This guide is divided into two sections. Section one is the teacher section which consists of vocabulary and activities. Section two holds all of the student pages, including assessments and graphic organizers.

Now available! Student Workbooks!

Find them on Amazon.com

Section One

Teacher Pages

Vocabulary

Suggested Activities

NAME:

TEACHER:

Date:

Chapters 1-10 Vocabulary

Relieved

Proud

Compliment

Nervous

Inappropriate

Sympathy

Consequences

Volcano

Deserves

Deployed

Coincidence

Optimist

Chapters 1-10 Activities

Reading Check Question / Quiz:

What type of party is Mrs. Hall having? Baby Shower

Why is the card Ally gives Mrs. Hall inappropriate? The card is a sympathy card

What does Ally show and tell about that represents her? A penny

Why is Ally willing to work in the notebook for Mr. Daniels? She wants him to like her.

Blooms Higher Order Question:

Construct a visual image, no words, that describes 5 things about you. Put the 5 descriptions on the back.

Suggested Activity Sheets (see Section Two):

Character Sketch—Mrs. Hall

Character Sketch—Ally Nickerson

Character Sketch—Mr. Daniels

Research Connection—Historic Coins

Draw the Scene

Who, What, When, Where and How

Discussion Questions

What challenges you have with school?

Predict what is going to happen to 5 characters by the end of the story.

What is Ally good at?

Do any other students have difficulties?

NAME:

TEACHER:

Date:

Chapters 11-19 Vocabulary

Apologize

Deserve

Conclusion

Interrupt

Adhere

Misfit

Fidget

Imply

Hypothesize

Immigrants

Invertebrate

Grudge

Chapters 11-19 Activities

Reading Check Question / Quiz:

What does Ally do when Keisha gets her flowers taken away? Shares half of her bouquet

What is surprise happens when Ally examines the box? She is the first student to guess the trick Mr. Daniels put inside.

Is Albert wearing the same shirt to class each day? Same style, different shirts.

What two other students does Ally become close friends with? Albert and Keisha

Blooms Higher Order Question:

Analyze what special talents you have or would like to have and what kinds of jobs these talents could lead to in the future.

Suggested Activity Sheets (see Section Two):

Character Sketch—Albert

Character Sketch—Keisha

Character Sketch— Shay

Research Connection—Ellis Island

Research Connection—Psychologist

Precognition Sheet

What Would You Do?

NAME:

TEACHER:

Date:

Chapters 20-29 Vocabulary

Enormous

Community

Seizure

Adaptation

Residue

Uncouth

Spectrum

Opinion

Explanation

Theory

Visionary

Scoundrel

Chapters 20-29 Activities

Reading Check Question / Quiz:

Who's party does Ally have to go to? Shay

What is the name of Ally's superhero? Roy G. Biv

What type of award does Ally win the makes her upset? Poetry

What famous person's museum does the class visit? Noah Webster

Blooms Higher Order Question:

In chapter 29 several "fish in a tree" examples are listed. Make your own list of 10.

Suggested Activity Sheets (see Section Two):

Character Sketch—Travis

Character Sketch—Miss Kessler

Character Sketch—Jessica

Research Connection—Bubonic Plague

Research Connection—Albert Einstein

Research Connection— Chess

Research Connection— Dyslexia

Lost Scene

Compare and Contrast (pick two characters)

Comic Strip (pick a chapter)

Advertisement

NAME:

TEACHER:

Date:

Chapters 30-50 Vocabulary

Diagonal

Incorporate

Reflection

Limelight

Invincible

Representative

Humiliation

Campaign

Persuasive

Observation

Analogy

Catalyst

Chapters 30-50 Activities

Reading Check Question / Quiz:

How did Ally communicate with her Father? By Skype

Who elects Ally to be class president? Shay, thinking Ally would lose

Who wrote the letter "from Max"? Shay

Who does Mr. Daniels agree to help at the end of the story? Travis

Blooms Higher Order Question:

Compile a list of famous people with disabilities (any disability, like the dyslexia list)

Suggested Activity Sheets (see Section Two):

Character Sketch—Suki

Character Sketch—Oliver

Character Sketch—Max

Research Connection—Senses

Research Connection—Stonefish

Research Connection— Abacus

Create the test

Interview

Top Ten List—Events

Write a Letter

NAME:

TEACHER:

Date:

Chapter Vocabulary (Blank)

Chapter Activities (Blank)

Reading Check Question / Quiz:

Blooms Higher Order Question:

Suggested Activity Sheets (see Section Two):

Discussion Questions

Section Two

- Student Work Pages
- Work Pages
- Graphic Organizers
- Assessments

Activity Descriptions

Advertisement—Select an item from the text and have the students use text clues to draw an advertisement about that item.

Chapter to Poem—Students select 20 words from the text to write a five line poem with 3 words on each line.

Character Sketch—Students complete the information about a character using text clues.

Comic Strip— Students will create a visual representation of the chapter in a series of drawings.

Compare and Contrast—Select two items to make relationship connections with text support.

Create the Test—have the students use the text to create appropriate test questions.

Draw the Scene—students use text clues to draw a visual representation of the chapter.

Interview— Students design questions you would ask a character in the book and then write that characters response.

Lost Scene—Students use text clues to decide what would happen after a certain place in the story.

Making Connections—students use the text to find two items that are connected and label what kind of relationship connects them.

Precognition Sheet—students envision a character, think about what will happen next, and then determine what the result of that would be.

Activity Descriptions

Pyramid—Students use the text to arrange a series of items in an hierarchy format.

Research Connection—Students use an outside source to learn more about a topic in the text.

Sequencing—students will arrange events in the text in order given a specific context.

Support This! - Students use text to support a specific idea or concept.

Travel Brochure—Students use information in the text to create an informational text about the location

Top Ten List—Students create a list of items ranked from 1 to 10 with a specific theme.

Vocabulary Box—Students explore certain vocabulary words used in the text.

What Would You Do? - Students compare how characters in the text would react and compare that with how they personally would react.

Who, What, When, Where, and How—Students create a series of questions that begin with the following words that are connected to the text.

Write a Letter—Students write a letter to a character in the text.

Activity Descriptions (for scripts and poems)

Add a Character—Students will add a character that does not appear in the scene and create dialog and responses from other characters.

Costume Design—Students will design costumes that are appropriate to the characters in the scene and explain why they chose the design.

Props Needed— Students will make a list of props they believe are needed and justify their choices with text.

Soundtrack! - Students will create a sound track they believe fits the play and justify each song choice.

Stage Directions— Students will decide how the characters should move on, around, or off stage.

Poetry Analysis—Students will determine the plot, theme, setting, subject, tone and important words and phrases.

NAME:

TEACHER:

Date:

Advertisement: Draw an advertisement for the book

NAME:

TEACHER:

Date:

Chapter to Poem

Assignment: Select 20 words found in the chapter to create a poem where each line is 3 words long.

Title:

NAME:

TEACHER:

Date:

Character Sketch

Name

Personality/ Distinguishing marks

Draw a picture

Connections to other characters

Important Actions

NAME:

TEACHER:

Date:

Comic Strip

NAME: TEACHER: Date:

Compare and Contrast Venn Diagram

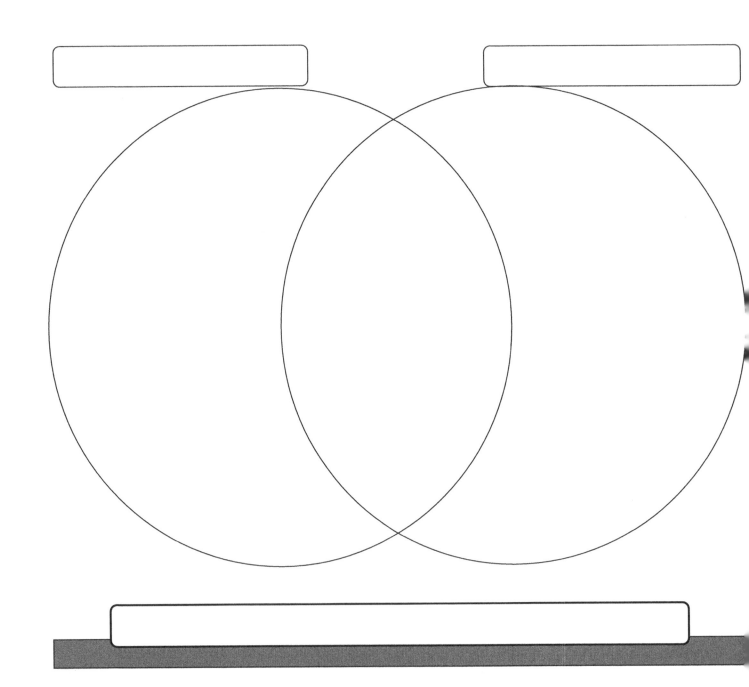

NAME:

TEACHER:

Date:

Create the Test

Question:

Answer:

Question:

Answer:

Question:

Answer:

Question:

Answer:

NAME:

TEACHER:

Date:

Draw the Scene: What five things have you included in the scene?

1   2   3

4   5

NAME:

TEACHER:

Date:

Interview: Who _____

Question:

Answer:

Question:

Answer:

Question:

Answer:

Question:

Answer:

NAME:

TEACHER:

Date:

Lost Scene: Write a scene that takes place between _____ and _____

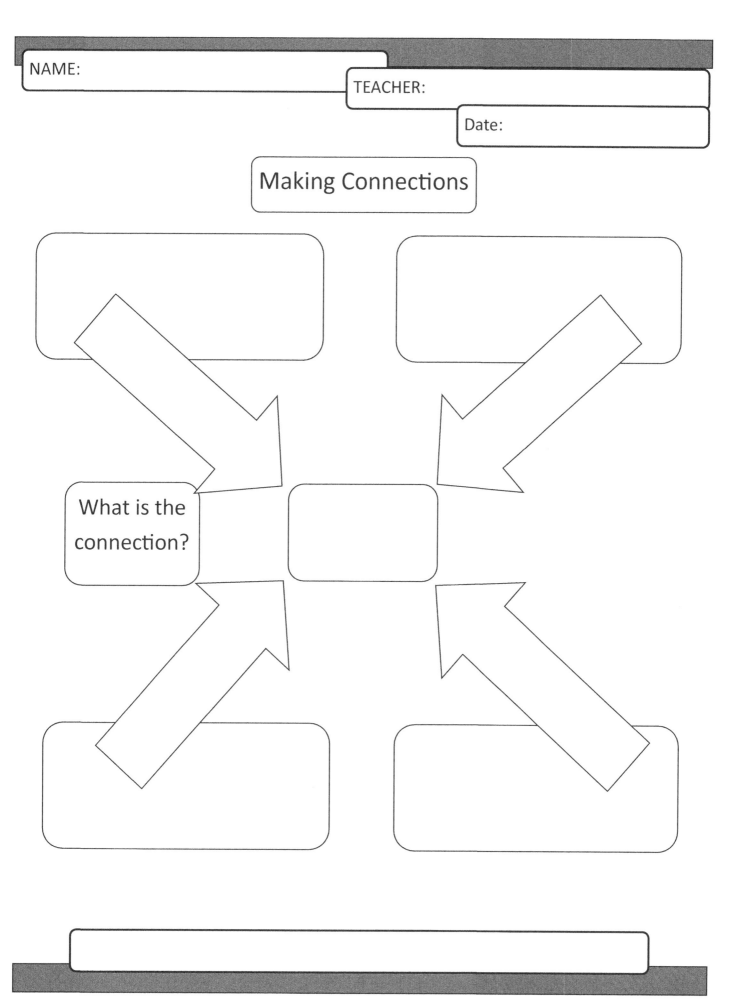

NAME:

TEACHER:

Date:

Precognition Sheet

Who ?

What's going to happen?

What will be the result?

Who ?

What's going to happen?

What will be the result?

Who ?

What's going to happen?

What will be the result?

Who ?

What's going to happen?

What will be the result?

How many did you get correct?

NAME:

TEACHER:

Date:

Assignment: Pyramid

NAME:

TEACHER:

Date:

Research connections

Source (URL, Book, Magazine, Interview)

What am I researching?

Facts I found that could be useful or notes

1.

2.

3.

4.

5.

6.

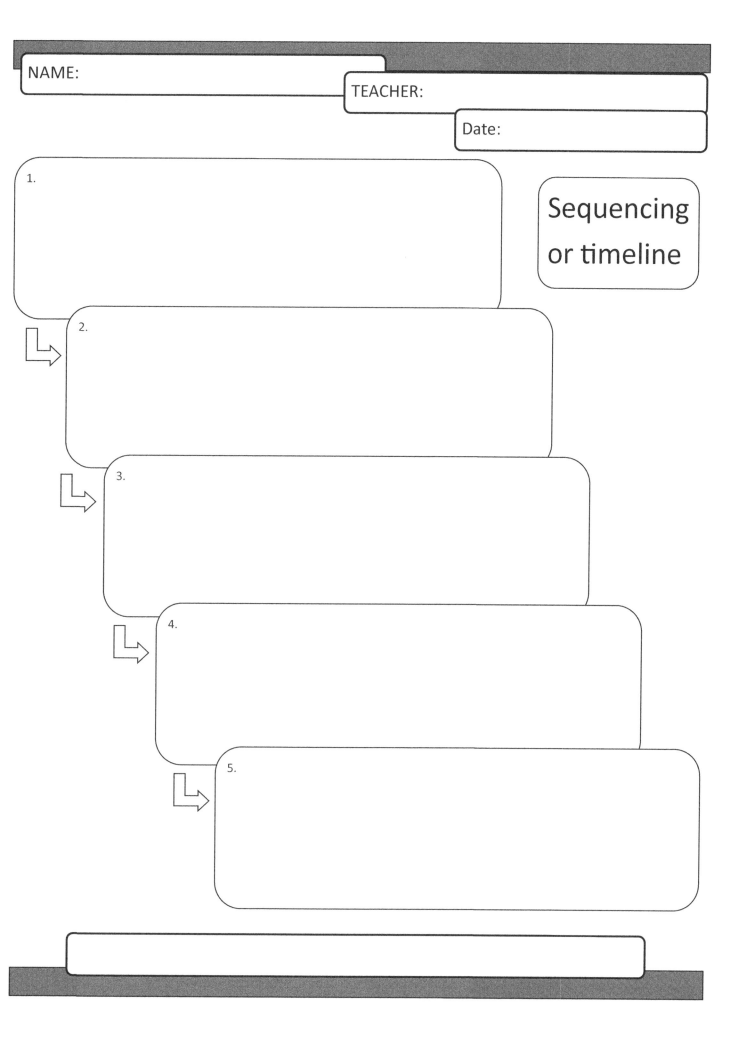

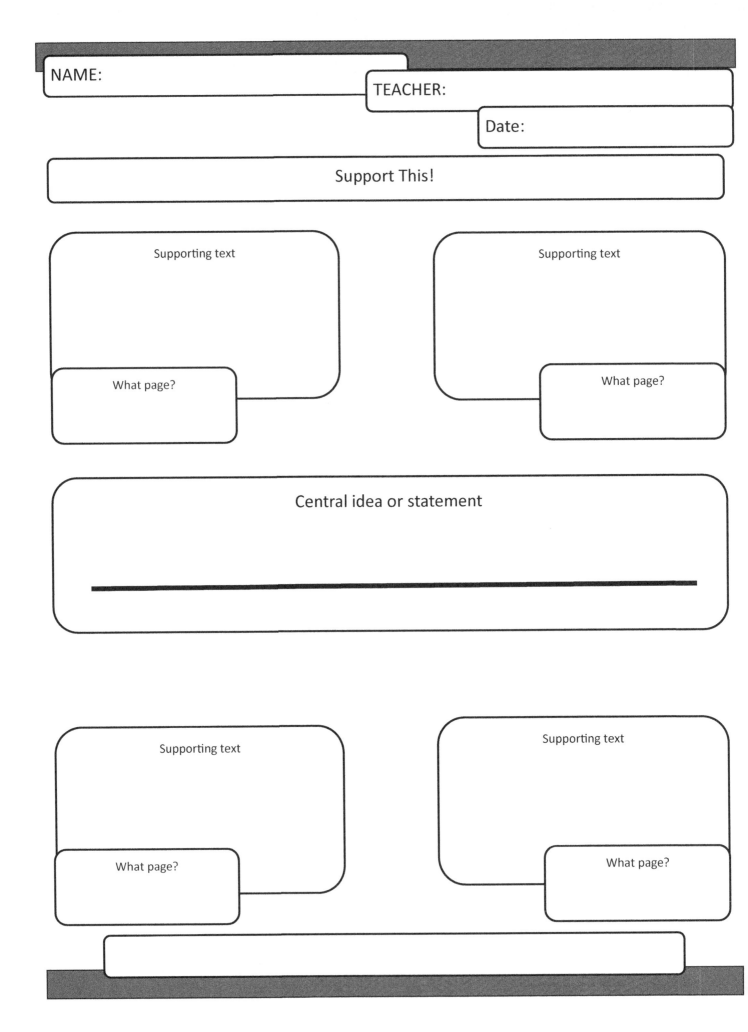

NAME:

TEACHER:

Date:

Travel Brochure

Why should you visit?

What are you going to see?

Map

Special Events

NAME: TEACHER: Date:

Top Ten List

1.
2.
3.
4.
5.
6.
7.
8.
9.
10.

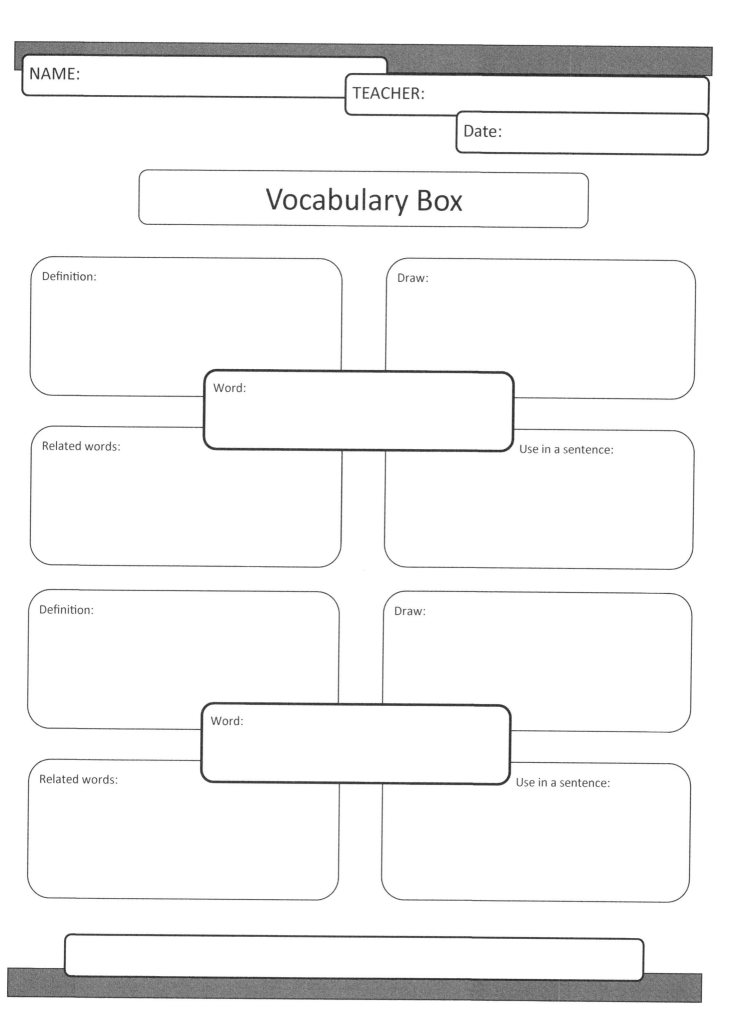

NAME:

TEACHER:

Date:

What would you do?

Character: _____

What did they do?

Example from text:

What would you do?

Why would that be better?

Character: _____

What did they do?

Example from text:

What would you do?

Why would that be better?

Character: _____

What did they do?

Example from text:

What would you do?

Why would that be better?

NAME:

TEACHER:

Date:

Who, What, When, Where, and How

Who

What

Where

When

How

NAME:

TEACHER:

Date:

Write a letter

To:

From:

NAME:

TEACHER:

Date:

Assignment:

NAME:

TEACHER:

Date:

Add a Character

Who is the new character?

What reason does the new character have for being there?

Write a dialog between the new character and characters currently in the scene.

You dialog must be 6 lines or more, and can occur in the beginning, middle or end of the scene.

NAME:

TEACHER:

Date:

Costume Design

Draw a costume for one the characters in the scene.

Why do you believe this character should have a costume like this?

NAME:

TEACHER:

Date:

Props Needed

Prop:

What text from the scene supports this?

Prop:

What text from the scene supports this?

Prop:

What text from the scene supports this?

NAME:
TEACHER:
Date:

Soundtrack!

Song:

Why should this song be used?

Song:

Why should this song be used?

Song:

Why should this song be used?

NAME:

TEACHER:

Date:

Stage Directions

List who is moving, how they are moving and use text from the dialog to determine when they move.

Who:

How:

When:

Who:

How:

When:

Who:

How:

When:

NAME:

TEACHER:

Poetry Analysis

Date:

Name of Poem:

Subject:

Text Support:

Plot:

Text Support:

Theme:

Text Support:

Setting:

Text Support:

Tone:

Text Support:

Important Words and Phrases:

Why are these words and phrases important:

Made in the USA
Monee, IL
11 January 2023

25088392R00026